Thank you

To: Kymirah

```
MW00325142
```

Continue to be the Queen you are! Everyday you wake is a blessing. You are legendary. smart and able to do whatever you set your mind to.

Destination Serenity

Daily Affirmations

Daquian H. Williams

GrindTime Publishing Group, INC.
COLUMBUS, OHIO.

Grind Time Publishing Group, Inc.
5440 Lonsdale Place South, Suite D.
Columbus, Ohio 43232

Ordering Information:
Quantity sales. Special discounts are available on quantity purchases by corporations, associations, and others. For details, contact the "Special Sales Department" at the address above.

Destination Serenity/ Daquian H. Williams. -- 1st ed.
ISBN 978-0-9831611-3-4
Library of Congress Control Number: 2021946758

This book is dedicated to my daughter Serenity
in whom I find Tranquility

"Serenity is not just an escape, but a precursor to acceptance, courage, wisdom, and Change."

–BILL CRAWFORD

Contents

Life is Magical

Life is magical and YOU are Worth Every Moment! I am a firm believer that every day we wake up, we are blessed. Life's spiral binding stairway has had its way of showing me many lessons teaching me to cherish all the people, actions, and moments created throughout my life. The moment we are created, challenges await our very existence before taking one breath in the world.

To begin creating our precious soul, spirit, and body, our mothers must first start to go through massive changes themselves within and outside of their bodies. Once we are called to enter into the world, we still have barriers surrounding every moment of the Mother's labor process to make sure a healthy King or Queen will be born.

I've listed 40 emotional traits or feelings because of their significant value. The number 40 is listed 146 times in Scripture; the number 40 generally symbolizes a period of testing, trial, or probation. We will overcome all emotions with the mindset of Serenity including:

1. Anger
2. Irritability
3. Sadness
4. Hopelessness
5. Social withdrawal
6. Shy
7. Lack of Communication
8. Nervousness
9. Fear
10. Sensitivity
11. Jealously
12. Raged at rejection
13. Physical changes happening to your body or mind you do not like

14. Thoughts all over the place difficult to concentrate
15. Vocal outbursts
16. Crying
17. Feelings of worthlessness or guilt
18. Why/what am I here on earth for thoughts
19. Impaired thinking or concentration
20. Negativity surrounding you
21. We are always arguing or fighting
22. Death Pains
23. Abuse
24. Abandonment
25. Lonely
26. Self-Centered
27. Judgmental
28. Narrow Minded
29. Lack of Motivation/ No Energy
30. Bullying
31. Disgust
32. Boredom
33. Shame and Embarrassment
34. Hatred
35. Confusion
36. Manipulation
37. Entrancement

38. Greed
39. Not good enough
40. Trust

Every day is a day to achieve Better Days. Conditioning the brain to do just that starts with you in the mirror every day telling yourself your daily affirmation for the day and completing the challenges attached to the day:

- What's better than success is happiness with me.
- What's better than material possessions is posing the mindset to achieve my passions.
- What's better than having an unlimited number of followers who give no light to who I am is to have love and peace amongst all that comes to my life and within myself.
- What's better than struggle, pain, failure, and feeling as if I cannot do something are the feelings of achievement granted to me when I continue to work through the adversities.

The paths I take in my life are much different from that of the next person. Life will give me opportunities through disaster, pain, struggle, high and low points to find who I am and my passions. Every day we will begin prepping our minds to start our individual journeys to conquer and reconstruct our minds to achieve greatness and find peace with who we are.

My Testimony

Please step foot into my story for a second as I place pieces of myself into your heart. Close your eyes for 5 seconds, clear your mind and thoughts, and then begin reading. I am battling impaired fragments of reality and imagination. Dreams of fun, laughter, and great times staggered by pain, questions, and hurt. Statements of remembering that time, or can you teach me interrupted by blood, tears, anger, scolding pieces of metal, and testosterone.

Walking up to the casket
My Mother ask, "You want to tell your daddy
bye?"
Three years old I reply, "Daddy feels cold."
The entire funeral begins to cry.

Three years old attending my father's funeral—this is my only memory of my father's funeral—one of many memories suppressed in my
head. Truthfully, I do not know too well if these
memories are real or just a memory a fatherless
child would create trying to fill those canyon size
voids deep inside. Far too often, the story many
young African American boys battle with today in
America.

At the age of three, my father was shot and
killed at 20 years old, leaving behind several single
mothers and a group of kids split apart from one
another. Just kids emotionally detached, being
tested through life daily, labeled a statistic before
even having the chance to prove to the world only
how bright the stairs are. At six years old, my
Mother was shot over five times. I remember sit-
ting in the hospital room every day after school for
days laughing, talking, and playing with this clas-
sic cup and ball toy, enjoying time with my

Mother. Memories of tubes coming out of my Mother's throat, nose, and arms become embedded in my mind.

Life lessons after lessons were reaching me at a young age. I saw pain, destruction, struggle mixed with love, laughter, and smiles firsthand. Nine years old, I am now hospitalized, having two vital surgeries on my appendix. My mother trading places with me enjoying our company, reading, laughing, crying, and guiding me through this detrimental process. My Doctors mentioned if I would've waited a week longer, I could have possibly died.

Trouble attached to me like a gang of lint crawling to some new black pants. I was a trouble magnet growing up, getting suspension from school, hustling, friends, violence, relationships, police encounters and even jumping forward some years. I took the wrong advice from a friend ending up with a bullet just missing my head at point-blank range.

There were thousands of incidents and learning points throughout my life, where my mind and current emotions controlled my actions & words.

Using earlier pains and struggles in my adolescent stages I began to make excuses for my troubled actions until 20. I learned just how bad words and specific actions can hurt someone and how the thought process of one can dictate their actions:

"You will never graduate high school."

"You will be dead before you are 16."

"Your Nothing in life."

"You're just another statistic."

" You are mentally challenged."

Just naming a few statements teachers, family members, and friends have told me negative energy hovered around my everyday actions growing up.

Born in Yonkers, New York, and raised throughout Columbus's Eastside, Ohio life touched home for me before I could even enter Elementary School.

My mother and I were faced with countless trials and tribulations that gave me strength and wisdom. My Mother continually feeding me positive knowledge, acknowledging if I am shedding my thoughts in prayers, and comforting advice that lets me know I can achieve all that I desire. Every morning asking me if I mapped out my positive reviews gave me the will to want to do better every day regardless of circumstances. Within those nutrients, my Mother instilled something deep within me.

My mother handed me a gift we all have inside. The ability to obtain wisdom and spread knowledge changing the thought process and actions of my daily agenda at hand. The ability to be humble always and love my brother and sisters. Strength to inspire others to be their best and greatest them. Endless amounts of courage and prayer to bring hope, enlightenment, and power to our nation.

Thoughts become powerful under the right umbrella. My Mother instilled many methods of empowering my thoughts, affirmations, and always making sure every day I knew how special I was. Establishing that mindset knowing I can accomplish anything I set forth to perform regardless of circumstances.

Through the miles of struggle, mountains of pain, and trouble, I am here today as a 24-year-old. I have gone on to become a High School Scholar and previous collegiate athlete at Notre Dame College. I graduated from Notre Dame

College with a bachelor's degree in Business, Political Science, and Criminal Justice. Chief Executive Officer of a 501(c)3 Non-Profit named "Better Days," where our mission is to break barriers and provide opportunities to underserved communities worldwide. Founder and CEO of an Early Childhood Development company called "We Got You Covered Nanny Care LLC."

August 2, 2018, my daughter Serenity Alliese Williams. Having a child honestly woke my mind up to society's dilemmas to an even deeper extent than which I was already attached to. I was utterly immune myself too. My daughter showed me just how endless love can be and if you continuously install positive wording into the mind, you can create a pattern that becomes part of your active actions throughout a day, week, month, or whatever the time maybe.

When I preach, please let your trials and tribulations build you as a person; please do just that you have the strength. Isaiah 40:31 says, "But they that wait upon the LORD shall renew [their] strength; they shall mount up with wings as eagles; they shall run, and not be weary; [and] they shall walk, and not faint." Allow your struggles to recreate the best YOU. Life is not made to be a crystal stair, nor are your Dreams supposed to dry up like a raisin in the sun. We are blessed through life's pro; regardless of where, how, or what circumstances we found ourselves in daily, we can create life-changing affirmations into our lives and those around us.

Children grow from pure love. Teaching children every day to conquer their emotional integrity can allow them to overcome many of the society of the negative brings.

Parents' negativity has surrounded you throughout your life. Let's all overcome together! Indulge deep into this great self-help, motivational reading you are about to begin! Spread your light on your children, neighbors, family, and friends.

Passion

Definition

A strong feeling of enthusiasm or excitement for something or about doing something.

Affirmation

My Passions can only flourish when my actions lead by example; settling for less than that is to set forth a compromise that I have not agreed to but opted into.

Motivation

"There is no passion to be found playing small--in settling for a life that is less than the one you are capable of living."

-Nelson Mandela

Today's Challenge

Take just 20 minutes today and list five things you are passionate about.

Name

Definition

A word or phrase that constitutes the distinctive designation of a person or thing.

Affirmation

My name shines morning, beaming rays of joy to who I am. My name is the first building block to who I am. I will always take pride in knowing my name makes me who I am. Names are not like the early 19th century, where everyone had a super common name. Now, names come with values to who we are.

Motivation

I am proud to be:

_____

(Fill in your name)

Today's Challenge

List 10 reasons why you are more than enough and capable of achieving all you set out to achieve.

Power of Mind

Definition

The mind is a complex element in an individual that feels, perceives, thinks, reasons, and gives one power is the ability to act or produce an effect. knowing the power of your mind is vital.

Affirmation

My mind is the most powerful tool on earth. My thoughts can turn into actions within the blink of an eye. I am an achiever and someone who overcomes all odds placed in front of me.

Motivation

Speak only of what you want in life feeding your mind with positivity only, surrounding yourself with people of the same mindset and drive.

Today's Challenge

Become passionate in wanting to learn factual knowledge and bettering yourself inside and out. Those five passions you have listed create five questions outside of your current spectrum of expertise. Research!

Strength

Definition

Strength is legal, logical, mental, or moral force a vital attribute or inherent asset.

Affirmation

I can, I will, I am as strong as the fiercest freedom fighters and carry the strength of a thousand kings and Queens.

Motivation

Why not you? Speak light into your life and those around you daily.

Today's Challenge

How powerful do you believe your mind is on a scale of 1-10?

- What made you choose the rate you chose?

- Where do you get your strength from?

- List five self-control methods for you to use during moments and times of adversities.

Definition

The range of one's information or understanding of a topic.

Affirmation

Knowledge is my key to unlocking the world around me. The more I know, the better I can position myself.

Motivation

Every day you should be enhancing your mind; learning something new daily allows you to think, observe, and act more with confidence rather than restraining yourself.

Today's Challenge

Write every day a list of 3 things you have learned about yourself, the world around you, and those around you daily.

Powerful

Definition

Having extraordinary power, prestige, or influence.

Affirmation

I am powerful beyond measure. What I set my mind to, I will follow through with actions. I am everything I want to be.

Motivation

Children are the blueprints on how to live life, soaking in the information they observe, hear, and surrounding.

Today's Challenge

Challenge yourself today to truly become a sponge to your environment. Go somewhere that you genuinely gain peace of mind and observe precisely what makes your peaceful place peaceful. The power in your mind creates beauty naturally.

Chosen

Definition

One who is the object of choice or of divine favor.

Affirmation

The moment I was born, I was chosen; I am determined.

Motivation

People may not always see the treasures of life God has placed within them. Treasures far more marvelous than that of the finest treasure hunts in the deep seas. They are often blinded by the words and actions of others, placing massive value in the negativity. Trust that God has created you in perfect image and you have been chosen and will always be chosen even when others are negative or overlook you.

Today's Challenge

List what makes you unique—what makes you who you are?

Extraordinary

Definition

Going beyond what is usual, regular, or customary.

Affirmation

Being more than average is exactly what I plan to be. I am extraordinary; we live in a world where many try to be someone or something which they are not rather than being themselves.

Motivation

Every day you wake is a day that you are blessed to continue living your life, becoming who you are destined to be. Keep your foot on the gas and you can never finish where you were previously.

Today's Challenge

List your happiest version of yourself. What progressive steps can you take to gain your happiness?

Definition

Having worth or value.

Affirmation

I was born worthy. I was made to be Great and humbling speaking I deserve the best from my life.

Motivation

If you feel you're worthy because of your be-havior, accomplishments, accolades, recognition, or any form of measurement defined by others you are scaling worthiness far too low. In that case, you create a sense of meaningless mercy to the will of outside people or objects.

Tell yourself right now they have no worthiness for you. You being precisely who you are and making the decisions you want to make is what makes you worthy. We are not perfect nor will we be correct every single time in our life.

You create your worth, and your worth does not come from something else and cannot be taken away from you.

Today's Challenge

Think about what our definition of worthy is.

- What do you consider to be worthy?
- Who defines your worthiness?
- How can you alter or keep those specific objects or people that we naturally feel create a sense of worth to our actions or stances in life from being the reason we don't follow our true self-worth?

Prime example would be if you are dreaming this but everyone in your circle is giving you negativity.

- Do you allow those negatives to determine your actions or enable those negatives to become your motivation?

Limited Edition

Definition

A rare asset, not easily found, only a few numbers uniquely created.

Affirmation

No matter what you call me or how you view me I am moving to my own waves, and I'm something beyond exceptional. I am the Limited Edition; there is no other Me.

Motivation

It's only one you. Think about it, is there any natural-born human in the world that is you exactly?

Today's Challenge

List all of the extraordinary and unique traits about you that make you a limited edition.

Opportunity

Definition

A set of circumstances that makes it possible to do something.

Affirmation

Opportunities come at random moments, many forms, attached with different levels of hardship however, opportunities wait for no one. Opportunities are not given in life; I have to take them.

Motivation

Opportunities in my life will come with my best foot forward. I know every day in life comes with a new chance to get better than the day before. Do not let an opportunity pass you by

Today's Challenge

List 5 things that happen today that could have led to new opportunities

- Have you ever missed an opportunity? How has it made you feel?
- What will you do to seize the opportunities?

Natural

Definition

Found in or produced by nature: being or acting as expected: born in a person or natural animal instincts natural curiosity.

Affirmation

We naturally seek love and acceptance; unknowingly, I can forget to be natural to myself and who I am. I will strive to be who I am naturally all the time. My natural self is more than a trillion words can explain. I am a natural-born leader.

Motivation

Love the skin, mind, and natural you because you are literally the juice dripping out the pot. Nobody can be you, but you.

Today's Challenge

Take just a few minutes and ask yourself a few questions:

- Do you enjoy who you are?
- How can you create ways to enjoy yourself more?
- What does it mean to embrace yourself?

Claim

Definition

To take as the rightful owner. Gain what one is entitled to.

Affirmation

I will claim my righteousness; I deserve to be happy, learn an abundant amount of knowledge, share that with those around me, enjoy the world, nature, and the ones that genuinely care to see me happy.

Motivation

Claiming everything I set out to accomplish, knowing I can speak light into my life and my body will naturally follow progressive actions.

Claim your life.

Claim your actions.

Claim what you deserve.

Starting Today.

Today's Challenge

Vision your life in every aspect, imagine your ultimate happiness, write it down, and read your dreams out loud starting from today for as long as you want.

Verification

Definition

The process of establishing the truth, accuracy, or validity of something or someone.

Affirmation

Search for verification, I am handling my business, following my happiness, and no one on this earth can tell me who I am or what I should be doing.

Motivation

We are living through generations where following the actions of others has become a popular trait to carry. Recognizing the negatives of being a follower can allow you to think freely. Nothing but respect for those listed below, but we live in a society where acting like somebody else besides being true to who you are.

If the Kardashians started wearing Sketchers, we would see a spike in sales. The Migos bring FILAs shoe brand back out; you will notice those who used to talk down on the brand in lines trying to get three or more pairs the first week of sales. Love and Hip Hop has the power to have some women eating raw eggs with chopped sardines claiming we're trying a new diet.

Today's Challenge

Authenticity last longer. Allow your passions to put you into new like-minded circles that challenge you positively.

List four different interests you have and find a like-minded group you can join matching each interest.

Recognize

Definition

Acknowledge the existence, validity, or legality of a situation or circumstance.

Affirmation

I am riding my own wave unleashing my full mind and becoming a happier person. I will begin to recognize negative paths and approaches that seek positive light.

Motivation

Specific people, habits, and ways of living will not match your visions, and recognition of those parasites like energies becomes vital to removing those levels of negative energies acting as fake superheroes.

"Get that Dirt off your shoulders, Gone head in just brush that dirt off your shoulders."

Today's Challenge

Ask yourself

- Are there people in your life that always talk negatively about life, those around them, or even you?
- Have you recognized negative energies in your life?
- How will you suppress those negatives?
- When a positive outlook comes about, are you likely to doubt yourself or take the path to see where it goes?
- What reason is worth explaining? Do you ever have to doubt yourself?

Tranquility

Definition

State of peace or Serenity.

Affirmation

Tranquility does not come easy living in a world where violence, wrongdoing, and manipulation are front running the news lines. Peace comes from within. At no time will I need to search elsewhere for who I am and my peace.

Motivation

The ultimate goal of therapy... it's too hard a question. The words come to me like tranquility, like fulfillment, like realizing your potential. – Irvin D. Yalom.

Today's Challenge

List 52 places, activities, or people where you can find your ultimate peace, and starting this week make sure to participate in one listed from your list every week.

Heal

Definition

To become sound, healthy, complete. To be made whole.

Affirmation

Healing is essential to the soul, mind, body, and spirit. It might be times where recovery is the least desirable thought in my mind. I will heal many times from relationships, social life, and professional reasons, adding in many of life's twisted plot twists to the occasion healing will become an important tool to reclaim my mind and actions on my path of peace, happiness, and fulfillment.

Motivation

You are alive, anything is possible! You are already defined in the Kingdom as one who is blessed and able.

Today's Challenge

Reflect on and ask yourself the following questions:

- Why is it important to heal?
- How do you heal yourself, finding your peace of mind after hardship?

Phenomenal

Definition

Highly extraordinary

Affirmation

I am Phenomenal, only I can stop myself

Motivation

"It is our duty as men and women to proceed as though the limits of our abilities do not exist."
-Pierre Teilhard de Chardin

Today's Challenge

Take this Challenge to your social media pages and have your peers get involved as well. For each letter pick a positive word describing who you are and post tagging #DestinationSerenity:

P _____

H _____

E _____

N _____

O _____

M _____

E _____

N _____

A _____

L _____

Adversities

Definition

A state or instance of serious or continued difficulty or misfortune

Affirmation

Adversities often lead to negative emotions. I no longer will allow struggles to decline my moods but use my pains as motivations to my ultimate happiness.

Motivation

"There is no better than adversity. Every defeat, every heartbreak, every loss, contains its own seed, its own lesson on how to improve your performance the next time."

- Malcolm X

Today's Challenge

Many people are just placed in your life to learn lessons. Surround yourself around fewer lessons and more blessings. Cherish those who celebrate when you are happy just as much as you do. Develop a network of positive people surrounding you that still can tell you when you are wrong.

Create that list of people. If you do not have people you feel are qualified then list where you can begin to create positive networks or outlets to help you grow.

Problems

Definition

A question raised for inquiry, consideration, or solution. Posing a barrier to progress.

Affirmation

My problems will never be more significant than I can handle. Relax, asset the situation at hand and know within the problem there is a hidden gem.

Motivation

Write as much as you can about everything if you don't like to write type, you don't like typing voice to talk. The beauty of technology is now giving us multiple ways to voice our thoughts letting our emotions be captured.

Today's Challenge

When you have a problem immediately give yourself 30 seconds to begin thinking before you react.

Analyze the situation at hand and all the possible outcomes

Evaluate those solutions to find the best fit scenario to solve your problems

If your challenging situation feels like it is not getting any better, restart the process using a different method.

You are not a Quitter and you do not give up when the road begins to feel like slippery ice.

Difficulties

Definition

Something or someone hard to do, deal with, or understand

Affirmation

My difficulties in life are ancient samurai iron steel swords sharpening my mind, soul, and body. I cannot look at problems as a hardship anymore but as a tool to strengthen me for the prosperous life ahead of me. Iron sharpens Iron.

Motivation

We must accept finite disappointment, but we must never lose infinite hope.

-Martin Luther King Jr.

Today's Challenge

Make a list of difficulties you have been through in life.

Now explain how those difficulties have made you a much stronger, wiser person and the process you used to overcome those situations separating the process by how productive each method is for you.

Self-loving

Definition

You have high regard for your own well-being and happiness. Self-love means taking care of your own needs and not sacrificing your well-being to please others. Self-love is not settling for less than you deserve.

Affirmation

I first must show myself the love, respect, and happiness I deserve. Self-love is next to self-preservation. I love who I am and admire who I am becoming.

Motivation

With loving yourself takes the first step into conquering your dreams and passions in securing a positive threshold over your mind once you love yourself you then can love someone else and spread love to more people show love to your companies and works of arts self-love is one of the greatest preparers.

Today's Challenge

Look into the mirror every morning now adding to your daily affirmation speak positivity into your mind, body and soul tell yourself how special you are.

Words

Definition

A unit of language, consisting of one or more spoken sounds or their written representation, functions as a principal carrier of meaning.

Affirmation

Words are powerful. One word can attach a life carrying message. Mastering the art of words not only enlightens me more but allows me to be even more of an effective communicator.

Motivation

Speak words of positivity and success into your life daily. Talk about your dreams to yourself.

Today's Challenge

We challenge you to a social media challenge tag our pages and #DestinationSerenity.

This challenge is a 30-day challenge where participants for 30 days straight post a short video a day speaking any words of wisdom to their followers they choose and challenging a new friend every day to accept the challenge.

Pains

Definition

Uncomfortable sensations in the body

Affirmation

Pain is much like history, we cannot erase, but we can decide to use the pains to ensure we will never endure such pains again.

Motivation

Invest in yourself, become what you dream

Today's Challenge

Find peace in God's Gifts that come without a price. Nature's works can be therapeutic. Go to a very scenic location near you and just gaze at nature's beauty, allow your mind to wander, and find your peace.

Listen

Definition

It gives one's full attention. To gain insight through hearing.

Affirmation

Listening is essential to my overall growth in any spectrum of life you can journey into, listening more I can begin to know what everybody else wants, needs. Listening to the words others say create endless lanes of knowledge for me to explore

Motivation

"If you always do what you've always done, you'll always be where you've always been."
-T.D. Jakes

Today's Challenge

When you speak to others, begin to listen to their full dialogue, in-depth practicing active listening skills regularly.

- What are active listening skills?
- How do you apply your active listening skills?

Separate

Definition

Apart or by itself.

Affirmation

My thoughts carry the strength of the strong-
est mammals to breathe on the planet. My mind
can pull 1,141 times the weight of the world!
I know this will be a battle and last a lifetime, but
I am willing to free my mind to live in Utopia on
earth.

Motivation

Daily you will be conscious of separating yourself from distractions, negativity, unsure thoughts, unwanted habits, and forces working against your growth's betterment.

Today's Challenge

Ask yourself and reflect on:

- What negative energies surround you?
- How can you rid those unwanted energies surrounding you?

Failure

Definition

Lack of Absence or Success.

Affirmation

Do I achieve real success without failure? If I am always winning, I never know what it feels like to lose to never truly value my winnings. I will accept failure for the lessons falling short will teach me.

Motivation

Even when you fail, you must find peace and happiness in knowing that failure will be a lesson that leads you through your triumphs, building your growth to get back up and better for the next round.

Today's Challenge

Ask yourself and reflect on:

- What is failure for you?
- List failures you have undergone.
- Describe where in the situation you failed.
- Speak on ways you could have made the scene better or actual won altogether.

Growth

Definition

The process of developing or maturing physically, mentally, or spiritually.

Affirmation

Growth comes at the expense of hard work, struggle, pain, and continuously strengthening my knowledge. Proper Growth will take me from my comfort zone into atmospheres beyond the stratosphere. It is not until I embrace those changes that growth can begin to blossom.

Motivation

Become comfortable with being uncomfortable—anything worth having or enjoying will come with a few obstacles.

Today's Challenge

Ask yourself and reflect on:

- What do I really enjoy in life? How can I manifest those joys?
- Am I surrounding myself around where I want to be mentally and physically?
- Do I settle for mediocre?
- What moment changed your life forever?
- What does your ideal day look like?
- What are you most afraid of?
- What are you most proud of?
- Have you witnessed yourself growing as a person? If so, where have you grown?

Emotions

Definition

Instinctive or intuitive feeling as distinguished from reasoning or knowledge.

Affirmation

My emotions are encased in the thoughts within my head. The thoughts wondering in my mind tug on me as a 3-year-old asking their parents for candy at the store. Handling my emotions first must be met with controlling my thoughts.

I am what I think, I think what I am is what I am. If I want to be in a euphoric state I must first align my mind to feel happy and lead shortly after I will act happy, creating a system of instilling the positive energy I crave directly into my mind, body, and soul.

Motivation

When we experience darkness, it is imperative to change our mood right away. Time does heal all wounds, and there is an acceptable time frame to process the upsetting event and feel the emotions altogether. However, once that time lapses, we must act and avoid negative emotions. Control You and Change Your Mood!

Today's Challenge

Find your Peaceful Zone. Find and List your outlets rather than a specific activity, place, or group of loved ones; you can be yourself, relax, and unwind your mind taking away those added pressures or concerns.

Definition

A particular opinion, belief, or idea about someone or something.

Affirmation

My thoughts are unmeasurable. If I think I cannot then I will not. I must alter my thoughts to think positively 24/7 turning any circumstances not of the best outcome into positive outbreaks soon to happen. My mind is powerful, and my thoughts can come to flourish.

Motivation

Everyday continues to build on our affirmations as you will add daily positivity into your life every day building lifelong habits. Find positive in all situations, even when they have initial adverse outcomes.

Today's Challenge

Knowing that nothing can stop you from being you by any means every moment and day you are blessed to be here, it's Go Mode. Write a goal a day in the morning that you will achieve.

Grind

Definition

The act of repetitive working towards achieving a goal

Affirmation

Every day let my actions self-educate me, frequently performing repetitive movements repeatedly to attain my goals.

Motivation

I am chasing towards my passions, dreams, and happiness every second I get on God's beautiful land. The only person who can stop me mentally or physically on this earth is ME.

Today's Challenge

How will I keep from overwhelming myself when grinding becomes such a repetition, you begin to feel like you want to quit? Remember you control what is attainable but to remain within your limits of ability, so you don't discourage yourself.

Ambition

Definition

A strong desire to do or to achieve something, typically requiring determination and hard work.

Affirmation

My Ambition is driven with a passion more profound than that of the greatest love stories. Dreaming for what many will consider not attainable, I will be uncomfortable with my present environment and achievements, never satisfied but always pressing forward to better things in the future.

Motivation

"For what is an advantage, if he gains the whole world, and loses himself, or be cast away."
-Luke 9:25 (KJV)

Today's Challenge

Ambition carries a strong desire to achieve something in life, however, controlling those ambitions keeping your mind positive should be your leading focus. Ambition gives us targets to reach in life inserting a sense of direction towards our goals in life. How will you leave your comfort zone today?

Hard Work

Definition

A great deal of effort or endurance.

Affirmation

Hard work consecutively will leave me in a better situation than I was yesterday over time.

Motivation

Your dreams will not begin to work until your hard work begins to become consecutive. As you

continue dedicating yourself to your passions
watch the noise your success begins to create

Today's Challenge

Ask yourself and reflect on:

- What is hard work for you?
- What is the value of hard work for you?
- How can hard work benefit you?
- How can you work your mind more to
  work your body smarter?

Negativity

Definition

The constant negative expression of criticism or pessimism about someone.

Affirmation

Every day I wake is a blessing, I will strive to better myself daily each day better than the last day. I keep all positive energy around me because of all negative energy regardless of its depth, person, place, memory, to name a few examples of negative spirits that can feed lousy energy until your soul. No negativity unless constructive criticism is healthy for my body, mind, or soul.

Motivation

To minimize the impact of negativity in your life, consider these scenarios:

1. I am avoiding "negativity " when others bring negativity to me.
2. Do not spread negativity to others when you find yourself in a negative mood.
3. Instantly think positively.

Today's Challenge

Construct a list of all negatives within your life. Now ask yourself how do you rid these negatives in a way that betters you and allows the negatives to harbor the energy elsewhere?

Combative

Definition

Being in a constant state of consecutive physical or verbal altercations.

Affirmation

If angered I will remove myself from the situation, find my peace, and focus on the fact that I woke up this morning. No one or any problem can move me out of my zone but myself.

Motivation

A negative outlet or mindset will never create a positive outcome.

Today's Challenge

When angry start to ask yourself:

- What truly got me to this point of anger?
- How did I handle the situation?
- Where can I improve to decrease my anger?

Confusion

Definition

Unclear in one's mind about something.

Affirmation

It is okay not to know something, but I need to find the right knowledge to redirect the unknown with not knowing.

Motivation

"Don't be afraid to be confused. Try to remain permanently confused. Anything is possible. Stay open, forever, so open it hurts, and then open up some more, until the day you die, world without end, Amen."

-George Saunders

Today's Challenge

When confused follow these 3 simple steps and you will be right back on track:

1. Accept the confusion, accept, and the feelings of "stuckness." We all get stuck sometimes being stuck was meant to successfully move forward in your progression.
2. Relax, Breathe and Practice Patients
3. Evaluate what you know, and acquire new knowledge

Manipulation

Definition

Social influence aims to change others' behavior or perception through indirect, deceptive, or underhanded tactics.

Affirmation

I control my mind and actions. If someone only takes from me, are they indeed supporters in my life?

Motivation

Ask yourself if this situation or person adds to my life and mindset or suppresses my mind and life. You will begin to cut off half your friends list before you know it.

Today's Challenge

Manipulators at work, within your social life, and family situations, once a manipulator succeeds in taking advantage of you, he or she will likely repeat the violation until you act. Have you felt used or used by someone? Why is it that you feel this way?

Trust

Definition

Firm belief in the character, strength, or truth of someone or something.

Affirmation

Trusting myself makes the process of growing myself all around. Building trust in others is a process I am willing to always give a fair shake to. Losing trust in others does not mean I treat them differently, but I merely manage my decisions and protect my actions. Others losing trust within me means I need to re-evaluate my choices, asking if they were in my best interests.

Motivation

Yourself is the best person to trust. No one will do exactly in your best interests besides yourself. Work on your weaknesses and sharpen your strengths. Continue to keep good faith and support yourself, reward, critique, and set standards for who you are. Be yourself?

Today's Challenge

Do you trust yourself? Trust yourself enough today to do something that you have never done before.

Dedication

Definition

Committing yourself to something or some-body.

Affirmation

There are no shortcuts to any goal worth achieving.

"I had to make my own living and my own opportunity. But I made it! Don't sit down and wait for the opportunities to come. Get up and make them." – Madam C.J. Walker

Motivation

Growing up, my mother instilled in me early that you get what you put in. If you allow spectators, outside noise, and bumps in the road to becoming a hindrance in your dedication to your goals they will do just that.

I will never forget the journey I experienced going through college. Feeling college was not somewhere I needed to be or even a place for a young man with my mindset. Football grounded me for a few years while undergoing financial stress, possible expulsions from school, feelings of mistreatment, and depression I had to make a choice. Leave and don't know what's next or begin to take control of my destiny dedicating myself to finish everything I start from there on out.

Today's Challenge

Ask yourself and reflect on:

- What are you dedicated to?
- How can you enhance your dedication?
- Why does dedication correlate with success?

Genuine

Definition

What something is said to be; authentic.

Affirmation

This generation has been furnished with tablets and cellphones, tarnished by celebrities, money, and material. I will hold on to those friends who genuinely care for me and support you through thick and thin.

Motivation

We live in a world where before you turn 13 years old I guarantee you know death, bullying, lying, and experiencing those controlled by ego. Having friends and family that genuinely care for your wellbeing, want to see you succeed, live life and travel with even a smile and cry together are vital to your growth.

If your network does not multiply your happiness but subtract and divide from your peace you need to re-evaluate whose energy you let into your space. It is okay to have a few reliable friends. There has never been a person telling you the more friends you have the happier you will be off.

Today's Challenge

- Ask yourself and reflect on:
- What characteristics will a genuine friend carry?
- Do you consider yourself to be genuine?
- Have you ever used someone or been used by someone?
- What feelings arise from such mistreatment?

- How do you develop genuine characteristics?

Improve

Definition

To make or become better, enhance.

Affirmation

No one is right all the time. Critique myself when I feel I've done my best analyze my failure to learn where my success lies, I can always improve I will not get complacent with being good because I know I can still be better

Motivation

Every day makes the next day better than the previous. Better yourself at one aspect of your life daily; do not discourage yourself. Trying to do it all at once can lead to conflict.

Today's Challenge

Write down the changes going on in your life daily and consider the opportunities you have to improve yourself.

Perspective

Definition

A particular attitude toward or way of regarding something; a point of view.

Affirmation

I will make it my mission to continue to sharpen my logic of perspective. Changing the mindset of which I look at everything happening in my life can ultimately change the situations I am looking at beginning to change.

Motivation

Looking at life from different perspectives makes you realize that it is not the deer crossing the road, rather it's the road that is crossing the forest.

-Muhammad Ali

Today's Challenge

Post a video or write a post explaining your understanding of another person's perspective and why it is okay to have different opinions.

Tag 10 friends to repeat your challenge and begin to watch how each story shines reasoning behind different perspectives.

Definition

The strength and vitality required for sustained physical or mental activity.

Affirmation

The energy of the mind is the energy of life, eternal peace and happiness I need to be careful with who I place my point into and what energy surrounds me at every moment.

Motivation

Vibrate positive energy into other souls and allow your soul to ignite positive waves through your life.

Today's Challenge

Take just 1 hour today and:

1. Practice Breathing.
2. Make Peace with yourself.
3. Think Positive.
4. Surround yourself around positive energy.
5. Eliminate all negativity.

Genius

Definition

Exceptional intellectual or creative power or other natural ability.

Affirmation

My mind is powerful, creative, unbothered by those not thinking on the same level.

Motivation

No one on this earth is stupid. We have moments of confusion and not knowing maybe even when we are misled and willing to battle our thought truths. From today on you will control your inner thoughts fully.

Today's Challenge

Tell yourself you are smart, a genius capable of the incapable every single day. Lessen your debates with those who are misleading. Finally, learn 5 new facts, talents, or any sort of knowledge bettering yourself.

Devote

Definition

Give all or a large part of one's time or resources to (a person, activity, or cause).

Affirmation

I didn't get here merely from my Mother and father. There is a higher power and along with devoting my life to my happiness and passions, I must save all of me to my higher power.

Motivation

"Now set your heart and your soul to seek the LORD your God; arise, therefore, and build the sanctuary of the LORD God, so that you may bring the ark of the covenant of the LORD and the holy vessels of God into the house that is to be built for the name of the LORD."

-1 Chronicles 22:19 (NIV)

Today's Challenge

Today take 30 minutes and devote your time to pure music of your choice, eyes closed, mind open, and relaxed in a meditation state of frame.

Revolutionary

Definition

Involving or causing a complete or dramatic change.

Affirmation

I am someone who will better the world, I am an innovator seeking to create revolutionary new changes to the world.

Motivation

"The most important kind of freedom is to be what you really are. You trade in your reality for a role. You trade in your sense for an act. You give up your ability to feel, and in exchange, put on a mask. There can't be any large-scale revolution until there's a personal revolution, on an individual level. It's got to happen inside first."

-Jim Morrison

Today's Challenge

A revolutionary person advocates change to the people and ideas around the world. Challenging the day to day progression or regression of natural order to achieve their goals. Make a list! What changes to the world do you want?

Venture

Definition

A risky or daring journey or undertaking.

Affirmation

There's no accomplishment without a venture; there is no venture without first facing the unknown.

Motivation

Venture into the unknown; many do not dare to go and begin to unlock passages of success although your life.

Today's Challenge

Take just 20 minutes today and describe where you see your life venturing these next two years?

Definition

Take delight or pleasure in

Affirmation

I must find peace and all things that do not go my way to find peace in negativity so then I can enjoy all my blessings thoroughly, enjoy the life I have in front of me and enjoy those I cherish in my life.

Motivation

"People rarely succeed unless they have fun in what they are doing."
-Dale Carnegie

Today's Challenge

List as many things as possible you enjoy about your life, try to go for nothing less than 25 listed.

Acknowledge

Definition

Accept or admit the existence or truth.

Affirmation

I will not turn my back to those who have always been in my corner, or even just arrived in my corner but who've always shown genuine support, love, peace and gave me an outlet to be who I am and express myself without judgment and only wanting the best for me.

Motivation

Acknowledge people for always being there for you rather the storm was in full steam or the rays from the shine where gleaming through with happiness. Begin to acknowledge the truth rather than covering it up, lying, or not speaking up for what is right.

Today's Challenge

Acknowledgment is the first stage of greatness. Create a list acknowledging any wrongs you may have committed, write where you have learned from the situation positive and negative.

Dream

Definition

Series of thoughts, images, and sensations occurring in a person's mind during sleep

Affirmation

I will dream for the furthest galaxies, light-years away knowing if I fail, I'm landing on a planet in another universe.

Motivation

What happens to a dream deferred?
Does it dry up
Like a raisin in the sun?
Or fester like a sore--
And then run?
Does it stink like rotten meat?
Or crust and sugar over--
like a syrupy sweet?
Maybe it just sags
like a heavy load.
Or does it explode?
by Langston Hughes

Today's Challenge

What are your dreams? What do you believe
you should do from an unsuccessful venture in
achieving your dreams? What's holding you back?
Meditate on these things!

Courageous

Definition

Not deterred by danger or pain; brave.

Affirmation

Success is not the last breath, nor failure vanishing, but the courage to continue to build oneself for better days defines you.

Motivation

Adversity can affect all of us, what we learn from our trials and imply to our actions afterward creates who you indeed are.

Today's Challenge

How can you challenge your weaknesses? Put yourself into healthy but uncomfortable activities. If you like to speak to people but never have, this is the section where you will put those uncomfortable activities you've always wanted to try.

Brain

Definition

The coordinating center of sensation and intellectual capacity and nervous activity.

Affirmation

Our Brains are little libraries filled with books waiting to be open. Dreams sit as pages wanting to be turned.

Motivation

Successful people are using their minds regularly.

*Repetitive thoughts create connections in the brain that quickly become intact into our minds. These thoughts move from conscious to unconscious ways of thinking and being. That is how we act on auto-pilot.

Today's Challenge

There are four central regions in the brain. The frontal lobe is the most malleable part of the brain responsible for decision making. The cerebral cortex or neocortex is responsible for our 'free will.' It stores 90% of our brain's neurons and manages information, attention, awareness, thoughts, language, and recordings of our knowledge and experiences. The parietal lobe processes sensory information, with the temporal lobe controlling smell, sounds, speech, and vision. (Angelina Zimmerman/ Inc.com)

Create a list that describes daily activities on how you can sharpen each region of your brain.

Engineer

Definition

A person who designs, builds, or maintains engines, machines, or public works to a high degree or level.

Affirmation

I am highly engineered. I've been built to last through all pains, adversities, shortfalls and sadness. I am born to lead, learn, and live life beyond my wildest passions.

Motivation

"Before I formed you in the womb, I knew you before you were born I set you apart; I appointed you as a prophet to the nations."
-Jeremiah 1:5 (NIV)

Today's Challenge

Take just 20 minutes today and ask yourself, "What is stopping you from being the ultimate You?"

Number One

Definition

A person or thing that is the best or the most important in an activity or area.

Affirmation

I am more than enough, my skin, my flow, my style, my smile, me, everything I do and touch is next level.

Motivation

I am becoming number one of my own atmosphere daily. I am in my own reign. Not cocky but confidently walking in the path of me.

Today's Challenge

Tell yourself daily you are number one and can achieve all. Create a list of who it is you truly are.

Family

Definition

A group of one or more parents and their children living together as a unit.

Affirmation

Family is those who love you unconditionally regardless of the situation. You may fight, argue, laugh, love, cry, share deep unclose feelings to one another. Family is who is genuinely there for you regardless of blood.

Motivation

I've lost so many people rather physically not here no more or even life situations spreading me apart from some. Losing someone always cuts nerves you never want to touch. Family is said to be those loved ones' blood or maybe not blood that is there for you when life moments are thick as honey and there for you when life brings you scenarios, not in your beat favor.

Tell these people you love them every moment you get to tell them you love them. Leaving yourself in moments where you feel as if you could not express yourself or speak your truth can lead to feelings of pain and regret.

Never let the situation curve you away from family or express yourself on how you truly feel. Treat every day as it is a blessing to be alive. Don't let a moment go by if you did not express your love to your family.

Today's Challenge

Tell your loved ones you love them.

Peace

Definition

Mental calm, freedom from disturbance; tranquility.

Affirmation

My Serenity is my peace, happiness, and no person or actions can break the bond I have created with my Serenity.

Motivation

If you feel as if your peace has been missing, take your time and inspect where you find most happiness rather than an activity, specific people, or even hidden places around you that take you away from negativity.

Today's Challenge

Take just 30 minutes today and ask yourself:

1. Where do you want to travel?
2. Do you have a place of peace?
3. Who brings peace to you?

Incredible

Definition

Challenging to believe; extraordinary.

Affirmation

Life is incredible, I am unique, perfect in the highest eyes, my mind is a diverse powerful tool, I will enjoy living this remarkable life I am blessed to have

Motivation

There is an incredible value in following your passions, showing positivity to those around you and building your communities.

Today's Challenge

Stroll through your neighborhood, enjoy all that is around you, and list ten new visuals or places that bring happiness or excitement to your soul.

Unique

Definition

Varied from the common, different in every way, an original.

Affirmation

To be different is to be irreplaceable, to be yourself and no one else is to be great; be yourself, you are unique.

Motivation

"What sets you apart often can feel like a burden and it's not. A lot of the time it is what makes you great"
-Emma Stone

Today's Challenge

Today will be the first day you never compare yourself to another person on this earth. You do not need to pretend to be anybody you not.

Admit

Definition

Confess to be true or to be the case, typically with reluctance.

Affirmation

It is okay for me to be wrong; admitting who I am and my flaws are the first steps to becoming who I truly want to be.

Motivation

There is no test more significant for one than that test of admitting when someone has made a mistake, messed up, or flawed in a situation. Are they capable of admitting their wrongs and correcting their wrongs?

Today's Challenge

Take just 30 minutes today and ask yourself:

1. Can you genuinely admit when you're wrong?
2. What lessons have you learned from being wrong?
3. Why is honesty with yourself essential?
4. What are the weaknesses?

describe where you see your life venturing these next two years?

Struggle

Definition

To proceed with incredible difficulty.

Affirmation

The struggle motivates me...being under pressure or in situations where many would bust or even myself in previous times.

Motivation

Perish all doubt, nothing on this earth can break who you are. There is no obstacle that you cannot conquer. Open your mind, clear your heart, and find the beauty within the struggles.

Ask yourself how I can overcome this temporary moment.

Today's Challenge

*Elevate your body.
Try something physically new for you.

*Prepare your mind.
Gear your mind to tap into the proper knowledge and resources.

Suffering

Definition

State of undergoing pain, distress, or hardship.

Affirmation

Suffering in silence does harm. It is okay to speak to my trusted communication sources when I need to communicate my feelings to someone.

Motivation

"We must learn to regard people less in the light of what they do or omit to do, and more in the light of what they suffer."
-Dietrich Bonhoeffer

Today's Challenge

What negatives can suffer in silence present?

What are the positives of communicating your suffering with a trusted individual?

List some trusted individuals or outlets you trust.

Tears

Definition

A brief spell of erratic or unrestrained behavior; a binge or spree.

Affirmation

Tears are perfectly normal. In fact, it tells me I have a heart and words cannot describe the amounts of sadness and/or pain I am feeling at this moment.

Motivation

Tears are messages from the heart awaiting the return of smiles.

Today's Challenge

Why is it essential to cry when the emotions or feelings match?

What hormones do emotional tears release?

Condition

Definition

State of something with regard to its appearance, quality, or working order.

Affirmation

Conditions will never define who I am or who I am becoming, and my conditions are memories to glance back on and smile knowing I made it through, and I've achieved my unthinkable.

Motivation

Never apply Terms and Conditions in any of your relationships; terms and conditions change into Contracts which can be terminated any time!

Today's Challenge

Condition the mind and body to practice excellence. Prepare a plan that encourages and guides you to become mentally and physically fit.

Patience

Definition

The capacity to accept or tolerate delay, trouble, or suffering without getting angry or upset.

Affirmation

I must remember life will throw branches at me. I may not have been ready to climb or even pick four-leaf clovers but patience, and perseverance will get me through all challenging obstacles. I will remain humble and keep good faith knowing Better Days are coming.

Motivation

You cannot be who you truly want to be until you take the time to free your mind, allow your body to follow, and begin to flourish. You were not born all in one day; it took time. America wasn't overthrown by the United States Corporation overnight.

Patience and a progressive mind are key.

Today's Challenge

What's the importance of being patient?

How do you keep patient when those moments in life or people become hard?

Discover

Definition

Find (something or someone) unexpectedly or in the course of a search.

Affirmation

In my life I plan to discover who I am mentally, physically, spiritually, emotionally, and socially every single day. I plan to discover more about the world, myself, those around me and become one with learning new knowledge about self and the world around me.

Motivation

Discover who you are every second.

Today's Challenge

Make a commitment to discover who you truly are and live life as yourself. Keep in mind that a large part of who you are is who you inspire to become. Take action to develop who you are—pursue an education, a career, a passion. Pursue your destiny as yourself.

Hope

Definition

I am feeling an expectation and desire for a certain thing to happen.

Affirmation

Hold tight to your dreams, every day is a blessing.

Motivation

"You may not always have a comfortable life, and you will not always be able to solve all of the world's problems at once but don't ever underestimate the importance you can have because history has shown us that courage can be contagious and hope can take on a life of its own."

– Michelle Obama

Today's Challenge

Hope becomes nothing without proper planning.

Let's take the first steps in your goals planning now.

What do we need physically?

Where should my mind be mental?

What resources should I tap into?

Mind

Definition

The element of a person that enables them to be aware of the world and their experiences, think, and feel; the faculty of consciousness and thought.

Affirmation

I will leverage my mind to create inner peace within myself and from outer peace following my passions.

Motivation

The human mind is unique in its ability to re-call the past, plan for the future, reason, and navigate complex relationships. Functions the thoughts, desires, and feelings we feel every moment.

Today's Challenge

Teach someone less fortunate knowledge you know randomly, allow your mind to expand. Challenge yourself to learn more daily.

Learn three new skills today.

Will you allow the matter to trump your mind?

Yes or No?

Focus

Definition

The center of interest or activity.

Affirmation

I will Focus on the possibilities of all my passions and dreams coming into full tuition and worry less of the chances of failures and not matching my dreams precisely as I vision.

Motivation

Lack of direction, not lack of time, is the problem.
We all have twenty-four hour days.
- Zig Ziglar

Today's Challenge

Focus on cherishing my loved ones, gaining more knowledge for your mind to absorb, build on yourself, social life, financial and happiness.

Allow good faith in yourself and your most high to lead you through the valleys and rivers ahead.

Fulfill

Definition

Bring to completion or reality, gain happiness or satisfaction by fully developing one's abilities or character.

Affirmation

When my heart is filled with endless smiles and passions of love and peace my dreams begin to fulfill my current reality. If I am doing what makes me happy, my ultimate success is fulfilling my happiness in my life.

Motivation

Color outside the lines lives outside the box. Don't let anyone tell you what to do or not. Don't be afraid. Listen to your heart.

Heaven is a state of being – of one-ness, and Hell is a state of being – lost. We simply need to live as we best define ourselves, find our own ways of being who we are in our world.

There is no requirement - only freedom of choice. We should not feel judged if we are doing what we think is best according to our perceptions at any given time.

Guilt should be discarded, moved beyond - what matters is who we choose to be in the next moment, given what we might have learned. We continually create ourselves anew.

Forgiving someone is a great way to show love and forgive yourself for the hurt you held onto far too long.

Take back the energy you have wasted on these things and reclaim your power to be your next best self.

Honor the past but refresh, expand, renew, fulfill. Heaven is within us, always reachable.

-Jay Woodman

Today's Challenge

What actions or thoughts bring you a sense of fulfillment?

Management

Definition

As applied to task. Task management is handling the entire life-cycle of a task, right from planning to tracking to execution. It helps teams track tasks from the beginning, setting deadlines, prioritizing tasks, and assigning them to the right people. It ensures projects stay on track and get completed on time.

Affirmation

Allocating time to achieving tasks I have set is of importance. Remaining organized, prepared, and prioritizing will better task results.

Motivation

Believe me, throwing too many eggs into one basket can cause an overload mentally and physically. Controlling your tasks at hand keeps the success of your overall goals in pockets reached at all times through your dedicated grind. There have been times where I've juggled too many tasks at once just to leave one of my focal points or multiples to suffer rather than being with family & friends, work, social activities, or even sleep.

Today's Challenge

Plan your days down on a written or electronic calendar.

Set days to contact your family and friends.

Set a social activity weekly for yourself.

Take your time.

Weigh the importance of your needs to live a productive life at the top and wants afterward.

Support

Definition

To give assistance.

Affirmation

I vow to support my neighbor, foe, that I don't know, and all in between supporting my brothers and sisters will come back in good faith.

Motivation

We all are connected through energy and supporting, strengthening, uplifting and inspiring
one another leads to vibrant souls soaring through
our lovely world.

Today's Challenge

Support two random people today, ten total
this week. Support another ten people you person-
ally know this week, along with those unexpected.

Control System

Definition

A Control System manages, commands direct, or regulates other devices or systems using control loops.

Affirmation

Control systems are what engineers my every action.

Motivation

"Incredible change happens in your life when you decide to take control of what you do have power over instead of craving control over what you don't."

-Steve Marlboro

Today's Challenge

How will you control your control system?

Knowing people are not controlled, you must key in on your mind to control your destiny.

Demand

Definition

An insistent and peremptory request made as if by right.

Affirmation

I am demanding the life that I want to have and the respect that I deserve. I hold all especially myself to the same standards of treating one another with dignity, respect, and kindness regardless of any difference that may set them apart. I'm demanding my happiness and peace.

Motivation

Create the world's demands that will strengthen, make our people wiser and bring humbleness, gratification, and sensitivity to one another's life differences.

Today's Challenge

Will you act upon the goals and passions for the life you deserve?

What do you need from your life?

Not want but need

SEVENTY-FOUR

Receive

Definition

Consent to formally hear; be given, presented with, or paid.

Affirmation

I am blessed. I never shall feel jealous or envy towards other people's blessings; with due time, dedication, faith, and determination, I will receive my blessings & stay humble as I appreciate and thank the highest for all that I do receive.

Motivation

"Always give without remembering and always receive without forgetting"
-Brian Tracy

Today's Challenge

We challenge you to give back, however you
feel best just make it a duty to give back somehow
today.

Establish

Definition

To make firm or grow.

Affirmation

I will establish who I am every single day I am blessed to wake. I will begin to develop the knowledge and foundation that will lay the stepping stones for tomorrow. I will establish my happiness, peace, and authentic identity every single day I wake.

Motivation

The Powers of Planning becomes vital, and you are becoming a master planner.

Today's Challenge

What makes you who you are?

Who are you?

Do others get in the way of being who you are?

What do you want to represent?

If you could create anything that would better the future, what would that be?

Express

Definition

Convey (a thought or feeling) in words or by gestures and conduct.

Affirmation

From today on out, I'm taking a vow to myself that will always remain within me everywhere I go. I will always express myself for who I am and what I represent. Even through times when expressing myself leads to what feels like I'm stuck in an oversized pot of quick sinking grits, I must remind myself that expressing myself is the truth to who I am. There is always someone like me or trying to express themselves somewhere in our world, me being me and doing right by who I can lead millions to do right by who they are.

Motivation

Far too often from young children we are told to suck it up or deal with it you can not cry in public, why are you mad and we suppress our real emotions, thoughts, and actions. I've walked into this story far too often. Lurking in the shadows of not expressing yourself leads to the destruction of you before anyone else. It is OK to express who you are, what you stand for, and the visions, passions, and dreams you have can flourish into real-life scenarios because there is only one you. Not expressing yourself can lead to depression and anger, feelings of being unsure as you allow others to write your journey following down a path to just listening to others, never genuinely catering to your happiness or mastering your dreams. I can recall countless stories where speaking my mind to individuals has resulted in positive experiences. Now saying these words means I am who I am regardless of circumstances; in stand by that, I will not spread negative energy and allow negativity to feed into who I am.

Early in my life, I had to learn I am who I am. I stand by what I standby, and I am a man of great faith, character, love, peace, and I don't like bullies, negativity, injustice, discrimination, or any form of wrongdoing to my loved ones or self. I've always believed in a fair shake and because of that young I became violent, argued, and thought with the eye for an eye mentality. Being rebellious to those who didn't respect my beliefs began to get me in trouble and ruin friendships; opportunities decreased because of my actions. Hence, I was the only one truly suffering, disheartened, and dismantled because the scenarios I felt violated who I am or what I stand for.

It wasn't until I learned to truly tune out the harmful noise, knowing I can live my life peacefully knowing what I am or who I stand for remains unshattered.

Today's Challenge

List 20 leaders in history that become who they are today because of being who they are then through adversity.

Vigorous

Definition

Strong, healthy, and full of energy.

Affirmation

A vigorous mindset to achieve becomes vital to the overall health and journey of MY LIFE.

Motivation

Overcome adversity; you have never bit off more than you can chew. Keep your plate nicely loaded with passions as the Grind continues; you will begin to attack your goals so much you have to restrain yourself from continually crafting your craft.

Today's Challenge

Post a positive video expressing who you are and what you stand for. Don't forget to #DestinationSerenity and tag 20 friends in your video.

Earned

Definition

To gain, acquire or get in return for one's labor, skill, or service.

Affirmation

What is worth having is worth reaching. All my hard work will allow me to earn all that I desire.

Motivation

"I've learned that making a 'living' is not the same thing as 'making a life.'"

-Maya Angelou

Today's Challenge

What do I feel like I've earned?

Has my work matched my earnings?

How do I convert my hard work into the proper earnings I deserve?

Unwavering

Definition

Steady or resolute, not wavering.

Affirmation

Unwavering conviction to my wildest dreams will convert to continuous action to achieve, better and better before I know it, my current positions will be trumped by tomorrow's "I made it through!"

Motivation

Don't ever let rejections or failures put you down and keep you from trying. Believe in yourself, have an unwavering desire to excel, put in your best efforts, persevere, and you will blaze your trail.

-Roopleen

Today's Challenge

Create a list of what you will do to help deal with feelings of being overwhelmed, unsettled, and distant from others.

Soulful

Definition

They are expressing or appearing to express deep and often sorrowful feelings.

Affirmation

Life is meant to be lived with soulful ambition, sincere visions for those around you, creating essential bonds to laugh, live, and love a million lifetimes over and over again. I have dragged through the quicksand of the past too long. Just ahead is a sandy paradise with a sun rising brighter than that of the horizon glow. Lift my head high, act from deep within, and allow my soul to lead me on this mystical journey.

Motivation

Once you are clear about what you wish to create, you can maintain a steady stream of thoughts – unwavering, resolute, and focused.

-Dr. Prem Jagyasi

Today's Challenge

Draw a picture or write a short poem expressing your feelings.

Alive

Definition

Living, simply stated.

Affirmation

What I feel on the inside rather than the emotion sinks so low sadness sweeps through your body or even joy of happiness there are many emotions that we face daily. I am blessed, I am alive, I am able.

Motivation

Do what makes you feel alive; become a master of yourself.

Today's Challenge

Are you alive, or are you a live strolling through the day to day motions?

Are you trying every day to better yourself?

That's all that matters. You will continue to better yourself every day.

Virtuous

Definition

Having or showing high moral standards.

Affirmation

Acting on good morals, values and filling my responsibilities lead to constant virtuous actions.

Motivation

How many times have I seen something or told myself that this situation or action is not right?

Today's Challenge

What does it mean to be virtuous in your words?

List your traits that carry virtue and list your characteristics that are the exact opposite.

Goals

Definition

The object of a person's ambition or effort; an aim or desired result.

Affirmation

My goals will be achieved.

Motivation

Your goals should be more significant than your person now. You should continuously be developing that mindset to achieve better every day. Your Dreams may be more significant than your current state now, but that's why it is your current state. Live in your passions.

Today's Challenge

Create a list of attainable goals you want to accomplish for the year

Create a 3to 5 year attainable goals list along with a ten year plan.

Humble

Definition

Having or showing a modest or low estimate of one's own importance.

Affirmation

Life has no guarantee of owl glass or point of the end; you never know when it could be your last day or even the previous day as you know it. Remain humble with every blessing granted to you and keep the faith, knowing no amount of

material, money, land, or purchases add up to
what will be remembered by those who love you.

Motivation

How can a man with no home, finances, material possessions live on the beach with his son, and
a picture of his sons' mother and his deceased wife
be filled with euphoria every breath he takes? He
loved the life he lives and cherishes every moment
happily with no regrets to the fullest extent?
Speak to everyone with a Prophet's words and
bring positive energy to all surrounding because
you never know who needs your positive spirit.
You also never know what that positivity can get
you down the line.

Today's Challenge

Write a short story of somebody who has had it
all in your eyes and then losing it for what specific
circumstances maybe.

Have you ever experienced such?

What were your feelings?

Where can you learn from that situation?

Needs

Definition

Essential or very important

Affirmation

I believe two sets of needs for my overall well-being are love, compassion, peace, and happiness. The second set would be the necessities needed to live a life such as water, food, a healthy mind, and body.

Motivation

The irony is that while God doesn't need us but still wants us, we desperately need God but don't want Him most of the time.
-Francis Chan

Today's Challenge

What is the difference between needs and wants?

What are your needs in life?

Secure

Definition

Fixed or fastened so as not to give way, become loose, or be lost.

Affirmation

Secure my feelings, family, friends, finances, faith, and freedom. If it does not concern any of those, I'm not going to allow it to phase me negatively.

Motivation

Secure your mind, body, and soul; you are on a jet stream trip to your Destination.

Today's Challenge

List your first steps to securing your feelings, family, friends, finances, faith, and freedom.

Acceptance

Definition

The action of consenting to receive or under-take something offered.

Affirmation

I do not live to be accepted by my peers or that of the mass society. Acceptance comes when knowing what & why something has happened.

Motivation

The art of acceptance is the art of making someone who has just done you a small favor wish that he might have done you a greater one.
-Martin Luther King, Jr.

Today's Challenge

Accept the things you cannot change.

Roots

Definition

Family, ethnic, or cultural origins are the reasons for one's long-standing emotional attachment to a place or community. The part of a thing attaching it to a greater or more fundamental whole; the end or base.

Affirmation

My roots define who I am and where I have come from. Accepting and embracing my roots strengthens my branches allowing me to grow taller and stretch more comprehensively than the world's tallest oak tree.

Motivation

Gratitude unlocks the fullness of life. It turns what we have into enough and more. It turns denial into acceptance, chaos to order, confusion to clarity. It can turn a meal into a feast, a house into a home, a stranger into a friend.

-Melody Beattie

Today's Challenge

Where did your family originate from before your great, great grandparents?

(This will take some extensive research)

Where are you from?

What do you come from?

Where do you want to go?

Who do you want to become?

Smile

Definition

Form one's features into a pleased, kind, or amused expression, typically with the corners of the mouth turned up and the front teeth exposed.

Affirmation

Smile there is nothing on this earth that can move me unless I let it drive me. A smile can save a life.

Motivation

The keys to patience are acceptance and faith. Accept things as they are and look realistically at the world around you. Have faith in yourself and in the direction you have chosen.

-Ralph Marston

Today's Challenge

What are the health benefits of smiling?

What are activities that make you smile?

Who are people who make you smile?

How can you apply these techniques to be happy and help you better through tough times?

Leader

Definition

A leader can see how things can be improved and rallies people to move toward that better vision. Leaders can work toward making their dream a reality while putting people first.

Affirmation

No amount of fame, money, or even material can define the leadership waiting to unleash from inside of me. Leaders come from those who strive to pull the best out of those around them.

Motivation

"I've learned that people will forget what you said, people will forget what you did, but people will never forget how you made them feel."
- Maya Angelou

Today's Challenge

List what qualities of a leader you carry?

What powerful vision of the future and unique business philosophy do you have in store.

Remember, hard work trumps all talent, and a clear goal and focus create a sense of success naturally.

Become innovative.

Understand the responsibilities and the importance of work-life balance.

Reinventing You

With every question, I want you to develop new ways of reacting to old situations, people, and problems to increase your chances of gaining control over your life and mind. Asking yourself these questions daily to develop positive goals, reactions to situations, and progressive actions. You may find that the "why me" types of questions won't feel unsure but give you proper guidance.

Knowing no one person is perfect, it is okay to align those gears that are not all positive.

What are the negative habits, traits, and characteristics you have? Your list can be as long or short as you need

Habits

1.

2.

3

Traits

1.

2.

3.

Characteristics

1.

2.

3.

Why does each factor written above exist?

What Positive habits, traits, and characteristics do you possess?

Habits

1.

2.

3

Traits

1.

2.

3.

Characteristics

1.

2.

3.

How can you align those positives listed to help conquer those negatives you have listed above?

List 4 personal goals

1.

2.

3.

4.

Explain how you will achieve your goal

1.

2.

3.

4.

List 5 Positive Outlets for you that you can access daily rather than a place of fun, art, music, activity, entertainment, spirituality, libraries, groups, gyms, etc.

1.

2.

3.

4.

5.

What're your biggest dreams?

List 3 ways how you can respond positively to possible scenarios causing anger?

1.

2.

3.

Where are the five places you want to travel to?

1.

2.

3.

4.

5

List 3 ways if you are battling with life problems and begin feeling sad or just not like yourself, you can make yourself happy, feeling back like you again?

1.

2.

3.

Do you have people you can count on to talk??

If, No, let's help build a network of positive outlets you can express yourself too. I want to be the first to offer you are always welcome to reach out via social media, email, or shoot a text to myself to have someone who will simply listen without judgment and only offer advice if you want it.

Have I learned something new today of importance to bettering my overall ME?

Ask yourself these questions every day and as changes continue to answer life obstacles you continue with good faith building your positive channels of thinking and empowering your mind and actions. Achieve your everyday goals, build secure networks, generate positive outlets and communication channels that will lead you to overcome roadblocks and negative points in your life.

Moving Ahead

Please Congratulate Yourself on your first 90 Days to your destination of Serenity.

You now have concepts of conquering your mind and placing yourself in a position to who you are, how you think & act, and finding your true passions.

You now have the essential preparation tools to know that your mind is powerful, and your thoughts can emerge into actions. You have completed Stage One of your journey to our final destination of Serenity.

The work we have put in is not done; we still have many avenues of the mind we need to tap into on this path to your ultimate you.

Volume 2 will continue from Day 91, teaching you exactly what you need to know to continue your quest to unlock your mind.

About The Author

Today Author Daquian H. Williams is both a successful entrepreneur and social entrepreneur alike. He is a college graduate of Notre Dame College earning bachelor's degrees in business, Political Science, and Criminal Justice. He is a loving and dedicated father who adamantly makes his daughter Serenity the focal point of his life. However, until now few have known that his drive for success has been driven by adversity.

Losing his father to gun violence when he was just three years old, Daquian's life was profoundly altered as he and his mother suffered countless life trials and tribulations. With his mother's love, guidance, and words of wisdom, Daquian conditioned his mind and body by enduring trials of pain, withstanding the struggles, and overcoming all the obstacles. Through life created learning lessons, blessings, messages and stages of growth and triumph; he has been divinely equipped with the courage, power, and passion to inspire others to be great.

Reflecting back on his life and the values that his mother instilled in him through daily motivations and affirmations, Daquian now shares his story and the secret to finding that destination of serenity that many who are broken and discouraged long for. When sharing about his life trials and triumphs Daquian often says, "Those early mornings and late nights filled my soul with ambition and eagerness to learn more and follow my dreams. Our minds and bodies can withstand, stretch, endure, embrace and achieve so much with the right drive." He now invites you on a journey—Destination Serenity.